AUSTRALIA
A PORTRAIT

The rustic life, Tasmania

AUSTRALIA
A PORTRAIT

Photography by Eduard R. Domin

Text by Peter Denton

CRESCENT BOOKS
New York

Looking towards Freycinet National Park, Tasmania

1988 edition published by
Crescent Books, distributed by
Crown Publishers, Inc.,
New York, New York, 10003.

First published by Little Hills Press
Pty. Ltd., Australia.
© Little Hills Press, 1987.

Library of Congress Cataloguing in Publication Data

Domin, Eduard R., 1958—
   Australia: a portrait/photography by Eduard R.
Domin; text by Peter Denton. — 1988 ed.

   Originally published: Crows Nest, N.S.W.: Little
Hills Press, 1987.
   ISBN 0-517-65835-6
   1. Australia — Description and travel — 1981—
— Views. I. Denton, Peter, 1955— . II. Title.
DU93.D66 1988
994—dc19   87—30096
                                            CIP

All rights reserved. No part of this publication may be reproduced, stored in a retrieval system, or transmitted in any form, or by any means, electronic, mechanical, photocopying, recording or otherwise, without the prior permission of the publishers. Such permission, if granted, is subject to a fee depending on the nature of the use.

Books printed and bound in Singapore.

ISBN 0-517-65835-6
h g f e d c b a

CONTENTS

Introduction 11
Photographic portfolio 13
An Ancient Land – A Young Country 95
The People and their Culture 103
A Journey around Australia 105
Map of Australia 105
The Land, its Flora and Fauna 111
Natural Wonders 119
Information for Visitors 123

INTRODUCTION

It is only two hundred years or so since Europeans settled the vast continent of Australia. The first settlers came in chains or as jailers but in time, others came to seek a fortune, to escape prejudice, to eke out a better life for themselves and their children, or as missionaries to tend the inner concerns of people and help create in the young colony a certain culture.

Australia is still a haven for some. Over time, concern for its own aboriginals has developed and the years of neglect and open hostility are being redressed.

This book captures in its text and photographs a unique part of the world. Unique in its people, scenery, vegetation and wildlife. The relatively late settlement has enabled the country to learn from errors of the "old world". Most ecological treasures are intact — the Great Barrier Reef, the wilderness area of southwest Tasmania, the awe-inspiring Flinders Ranges — thanks to an articulate and sophisticated lobby able to convey its message to a responsive government.

Rich in natural resources, Australia has a high standard of living, universal education and a stable social fabric. Its few people (only 15.5 million) have a charmed existence compared to some other nations. It has inherited an ordered and effective public administration and an approach to life that is akin to the Mediterranean countries. It is a place with much to offer, where the mediocre can survive and the hardworking prosper.

The discerning visitor will find that the Information for Visitors in this work will quickly put at rest any concerns that may inhibit their desire to visit the land "down under".

Tasman Peninsula,
Tasmania

The convict prison of Port Arthur, Tasmania, built in the 1790s

*S*unrise
*from K*irribilli, Sydney

*T*hredbo Creek,
Snowy Mountains,
Australian Alps

*Indooroopilly
Railway bridge,
Queensland*

The boiling cauldron of the Southern Ocean

*A*irlie Beach,
Queensland

*W*arners Bay Lighthouse,
Sydney

*M*orning
on Sydney Harbour

28

A fishing Trawler,
Western Australia

*Q*ueensland
canefields

*T*ropical
rainforest

*Sugar cane burnoff,
Queensland*

*A*n English meadow?
Tasmania

Great Western Tiers,
Mount Commings National Park,
Tasmania

*C*allistemon Cascades,
*E*ungella National Park,
Queensland

Finch Hatton Creek

*Broken River,
Eungella National Park,
Queensland*

*S*andbars near Eagle Hawk Neck, Tasman peninsular

*B*ogong National Park, Victoria

*M*ersey Valley,
Tasmania

*N*ariel Creek
after flood, Victoria

*B*risbane's
*central business
district*

Stockmen, Northern Australia

*S*ugar cane train,
Queensland

*D*evil's Gullet,
Central Plateau,
Tasmania

*L*ight snow
on the Central Plateau,
Tasmania

*S*talagmite and
stalactite formations
in the Naracoorte Caves,
South Australia

The 'Twelve Apostles' at sunset, Victoria

*C*edar Creek,
Queensland

*N*orfolk Bay,
Tasmania

*B*ronte cliffs,
Sydney

*T*hredbo Valley,
New South Wales

The Australian Alps

Canberra

Canberra

*S*erenity

*B*ogong high plains,
Victoria

*Brisbane
– old and new,
Queensland*

*W*illiam Jolly bridge,
Brisbane

A seeming tangle
of car lanes – Riverside Expressway,
Brisbane

71

Shute Harbour, Queensland

Tasmania

Tasmania

*F*arm Cove, Sydney

Smallys Beach,
Cape Hillsborough National Park,
Queensland

The Tasman sea from Warner's Bay, Sydney

*S*ydney's cityscape
at sunset

*S*nowy Mountains
Australian Alps

A cattle chute on a property, eastern Australia

*L*akes
in the Mount Arapiles area,
Victoria

*T*he Derwent River glides past New Norfolk, Tasmania

*T*he sun sets
Brisbane

Brisbane's pride, the Captain Cook Bridge

*O*ne of
Sydney's symbols at sunset,
the Harbour Bridge

An Ancient Land – A Young Nation

THE 1980S IS THE DECADE in which Australians are celebrating two hundred years of modern settlement. Yet the history of the land and its people predates this by many thousands of years.

Australia has the oldest record of life on earth – the fossil reefs at North Pole in Western Australia have been dated at 3500 million years old. It was not until about 225 million years ago, though, that Australia became a unique region of animal and plant evolution. This was because of Australia's gradual isolation from the other continents of the great southern landmass called Gondwanaland. Many of Australia's unusual animals such as the platypus and the echidna are thought to have survived because of the secure evolutionary conditions created by this long separation from the competing species of Africa, India and South America.

Many anthropologists believe the first humans to reach Australia were migrants from the northern Asian subcontinent. It is thought that these people arrived about 40 000 years ago and that 20 000 years later most mainland areas were inhabited. By the time the first European settlers arrived in 1788 there were an estimated 300 000 to 500 000 Aborigines in mainland Australia, in about 600 tribal groups.

The ancestors of the Australian Aborigine lived by food gathering and hunting, fashioning tools of wood, bone and natural fibres, shell and stone. Their culture found expression in a complex spiritual relationship with their environment.

It is impossible to date the first European contact with the Australian coast. Some historians believe that the Portuguese sailed down the eastern coast during the 1500s, but the evidence is to date only circumstantial. The first recorded visit was by the Dutch sea captain Willem Jansz, who landed on the west of Cape York Peninsula in the continent's north in 1606.

The early European explorers were drawn by the riches of the Eastern spice trade and the search for the mysterious Great South Land. As early as the second century AD the Graeco–Egyptian astronomer Ptolemy had suggested the existence of a vast continent in the southern hemisphere, somewhere to the east of Africa. But it was not until the end of the fifteenth century that improvements in shipbuilding, navigational aids and cartography opened the route to the East.

The establishment of Dutch trading posts in what is now Indonesia led to the charting of the northern and western Australian coastlines, as expeditions were sent in search

Impressions
of Sydney Harbour from
students at the Japanese School

of the legendary riches of the Great South Land. Among the many voyages of discovery were those of the Dutch navigator Dirk Hartog who in 1616 landed on an island in Shark's Bay off the Western Australian coast. In 1642 another Dutchman, Abel Tasman, discovered and named Van Diemen's Land to the south of the Australian mainland, but failed to establish that it was an island; it was later renamed Tasmania. On a second voyage, in 1644, Tasman charted sections of the northern coastline and gave the region the name *Nova Hollandia*, or New Holland. Primarily interested in trade, however, the Dutch found little in this new land to interest them.

The first recorded English visitor was the buccaneer and pirate William Dampier, who anchored in Shark's Bay in January 1688. In his account of this voyage, published in London in 1697, he described the country as harsh and uncompromising but speculated that in such a vast area there might well be 'fruitful lands'.

The discovery and charting of the eastern coastline of Australia did not take place for another eighty years. In August 1768 Lieutenant James Cook set sail from Plymouth, England, in command of a converted collier, the *Endeavour*. The primary task of his voyage was to observe the transit of the planet Venus, which it had been calculated would be visible from the Pacific island of Tahiti in June 1769. But Cook also carried orders which were to remain sealed until the astronomical observations had been completed; these instructed him to sail southward as far as latitude 40 degrees, then west, in search of the Great South Land.

In October 1769 Cook sighted the north island of New Zealand and spent the next six months charting the coastline before sailing westward. On 20 April 1770 Lieutenant Zachary Hicks, a member of Cook's crew, became the first European known to have sighted the east coast of Australia.

Over the next four months Cook sailed northward charting the eastern coastline, and in August 1770 he claimed the land for the British crown, naming it New South Wales. Cook's impressions were highly favourable and his reports described the region as fertile and suitable for settlement.

It was another eighteen years before settlement took place. England, meanwhile, was undergoing a period of complex social and economic change. Laws were harsh and the success of the American War of Independence meant that convicts could no longer be sent across the Atlantic to work in the southern plantations. A new settlement, secure and self sustaining, had to be found.

In 1787 a retired naval officer, Captain Arthur Phillip, was assigned the task of transporting 564 male and 192 female convicts to the shores of New South Wales. The First Fleet consisted of two warships, three storeships and six transports carrying the prisoners. It took eight months to reach what was regarded as the utter extremity of the globe.

Although the first settlement was located

on the shores of one of the finest natural harbours in the world, the early years of the colony were hard. Farming the unfamiliar land was difficult, and the recurring influx of more convict fleets carrying few supplies of their own stretched the colonial administration to the limit. Many of the first settlers died from starvation and scurvy.

By the turn of the nineteenth century material life had started to improve among the colony's 6000 inhabitants. Houses and public buildings had been erected and food was being produced on small farms around Sydney and along the nearby Hawkesbury River. The administration, however, had become a shambles. The dominant power in the new colony was a group of free settlers and early entrepreneurs, mainly officers of the New South Wales Corps, who were keen to exploit the convicts as slave labour and to monopolise commerce within the colony.

Rum had become the major currency of trade, controlled by the NSW Corps. In 1808 the activities of this group culminated in the incident known as the Rum Rebellion. On 26 January officers of the NSW Corps combined with a number of prominent citizens to depose the colonial governor, William Bligh, who is more famous perhaps for his role in an earlier mutiny, on his ship the *Bounty*. Bligh had been attempting to curb the traffic in rum since his arrival in the colony in 1806. He was forced to return to London where the leaders of the rebellion were later prosecuted. Legitimate government was not restored to the colony until 1810, with the arrival of Governor Lachlan Macquarie.

Over the next thirty years, as explorers pushed deeper inland discovering fertile grazing country, word spread of the opportunities that existed for those willing to take up the challenge. A new breed of energetic farmers, many of them emancipated convicts, began the trek inland with their small herds of sheep and cattle. Others loaded their waggons with goods and supplies and opened up trading posts to service the new communities. The rush for land, which was to last into the 1870s, was on. The most successful of these new agricultural entrepreneurs illegally took up huge tracts of unsurveyed crown land and began developing a prosperous wool and cattle industry. Over time, and because of the considerable economic power they eventually wielded, they became known as the 'squattocracy'. During the nineteenth and early twentieth centuries they were the closest Australia had to a ruling class.

The discovery of gold in New South Wales and Victoria in the 1850s received dramatic publicity in Europe and North America, and before long the docks of Melbourne and Sydney were full of ships and adventurers from all over the world. In the colonies themselves, town workers and farm labourers alike dropped tools and headed to the goldfields, often pushing all their worldly goods in a wheelbarrow or rolling them along in a barrel. In the ten years between 1850 and 1860 the population of Australia increased from a little over

400 000 to more than one million. Included among the newcomers were thousands of Chinese, many of whom despite often hostile resistance from the Europeans prospered on the goldfields.

It was a period of great change and growth for Australia. Fortunes were made and lost both on the goldfields and in the bars which surrounded them. Some of the money was spent on lavish buildings in goldmining towns like Ballarat and Bathurst, many of which were abandoned when the gold ran out. The wealth of the era also revived the practice of bushranging – bailing up coaches or carrying out raids on homesteads in search of gold, money or stock. Many of the more daring of these bushrangers, notably Ben Hall, 'Mad' Morgan, Captain Thunderbolt and Ned Kelly, have since achieved immortality as Australian folk heroes.

Australia's new wealth, based primarily on agriculture and mining, brought with it a growing desire for political independence. Back in Britain, the government was finding direct administrative responsibilty for the six colonies increasingly complex and expensive. This culminated in the granting of self-government to most of the colonies during the 1850s: New South Wales, Victoria and Tasmania in 1855, South Australia in 1856, and Queensland in 1859. Western Australia did not achieve responsible government until 1890. Independent parliaments modelled on the Westminster two-house system were established in each state, with governors representing the interests of the home country, Britain.

Over the next fifty years each state ruthlessly pursued its own social and economic interests as if it were a separate country. The main protagonists were New South Wales, which pursued a policy of free trade, and Victoria, which took a highly protectionist stance to assist its budding manufacturing industries.

The Federation movement began developing in the 1880s in response to the desire of the more longsighted citizens to overcome such individualistic policies. Besides dealing with intercolonial barriers to trade, there was a need for national defence and immigration policies.

Federation of the six states into the Commonwealth of Australia finally took place on 1 January 1901, the first day of the first month of the first year of the twentieth century. The powers of the federal and state governments were defined by a constitution, with the former taking responsibility for defence, external affairs, overseas trade, customs and excise, communications, treasury, social services and immigration. The federal government was allocated mutual responsibility with the individual states for areas including education, agriculture, energy services, health and law enforcement. Australia had achieved 'nationhood'.

The history of Australia during the twentieth

century has seen its expanding role in world affairs.

During the First World War Australia sent over 330 000 troops to the aid of Britain and its allies; casualties were 60 284 deaths and 152 171 wounded. The Australian and New Zealand Army Corps (ANZAC) is primarily associated with the Gallipoli campaign of 1915, when Allied forces attempted to push through the Turkish lines and link up with the Russian troops to the east. Although the Allies were ultimately defeated in their objectives, losses were severe and the date of the initial landing at Gallipoli, 25 April 1915, has been commemorated since 1916 in honour of Australian participation in all wars, including those before 1914. Australians also saw service elsewhere in the Middle East, and in Europe and New Guinea.

In the 1920s Australians enjoyed relative peace and prosperity due to the profit from the sale of commodities, mainly wool and wheat, in demand on world markets. But government and business interests were borrowing heavily from England and the United States to finance Australia's rapid development. Towards the end of the decade commodity prices plummeted and, with a high level of debt to contend with, Australia suddenly found itself in serious economic difficulty.

Like the rest of the world, Australia entered the 1930s in the midst of the Great Depression. By 1932, the worst year, nearly one third of the workforce was unemployed, while wages fell to 80 per cent of the 1928–29 level. Thousands left the cities and went to the country in what was usually a vain attempt to find work. 'Humping the bluey', it was called, as these swagmen tramped from place to place carrying nothing more than a billy in which to brew tea and a bedroll slung over their backs.

The Australian economy did not begin to recover and export prices steadily to increase until 1934. Five years later Britain declared war on Germany. It was symbolic of the nation's still close attachment to the 'home country' that within a few hours of Britain's decision the Australian government decided to follow suit. Yet this was the war that first saw Australia turn to the United States for assistance in its defence.

Almost one million Australians were mobilised for the war effort during the period 1939–45, of whom 27 073 died or were killed in action. Many more were wounded or taken prisoner in the wars against Japan and Germany. It was the entry of the Japanese into the war in 1941, and the extension of the conflict into the Pacific, that caused the Australian government to rethink its traditional alliances. After the fall of Singapore in 1942, and the bombing of Darwin and other northern towns by Japanese aeroplanes, the Australian government finally endorsed the view that its primary duty lay in the defence of Australia and not simply in support for the Allies in Europe. To the chagrin of the British, two Australian divisons were brought home from the Middle East and closer cooperation was sought with the United States.

In 1942, General Douglas MacArthur, commander of the United States forces in the Pacific, transferred his headquarters to Australia. Over the next three years the combined forces of both countries succeeded in pushing back the Japanese advance through Southeast Asia and the Pacific region.

Australia emerged from the war with a greater awareness of where its future allegiances should lie. Despite the predominance of those of British descent in the population, the weakness of the British pound and the strength of the American dollar assisted the swing towards the United States. Immigration policies also began to break down the traditional ties with the 'home country'. A larger population – for the purposes of defence – became a priority as Australians recovered from the shock of the near-invasion from Japan. The war had also created a much higher level of industrialisation, with an accompanying demand for labour.

Australia signed pacts with Britain in 1946 and the United States in 1947 providing assisted-passage schemes for ex-service men and women; this was later extended to members of the Resistance movements of a number of European countries. Australia also became a home for refugees from Europe, or 'displaced' persons – in 1947–52 nearly 180 000 were resettled. During the 1950s further arrangements for assisted immigration were made with many European countries and the United States. Not until that decade, however, was the entry of non-white migrants to Australia eased. And it was not until the traditional European supply of immigrants began to diminish in the late 1960s that Asia became a significant source of new settlers.

One of the major characteristics of the past forty years has been the dramatic effect the post-war wave of immigration has had on Australian industry, culture and lifestyles. Of the present population of nearly 16 million, roughly one in four is either a migrant or the child of a migrant; in 1947, only 9.8 per cent of the country's 7.5 million inhabitants had been born outside Australia.

Because of strong economic growth during the 1950s and 1960s, Australians began to enjoy one of the highest standards of living in the world. Unparalleled opportunities existed for those with the willingness and determination to 'have a go'. Strong industrial growth in the cities, and the continuing exploration for and discovery of vast mineral deposits of iron, nickel, bauxite, coal, oil and natural gas provided much of the incentive.

Australia also underwent a period of political upheaval during the 1960s with, among other issues, the government's decision to support the United States in the Vietnam War proving particularly contentious. The community was strongly divided on this question and, following the election of a federal Labour government in 1972, Australian troops were withdrawn from the conflict.

Australia is entering the latter part of the 1980s with both trepidation and excitement. The value of the Australian currency fell dramatically during 1986 as world prices for many Australian exports declined. The country has also had to cope with the rapid technological changes of the last decade, and advances that have been made in industrial efficiency have often been offset by high levels of unemployment.

On the other hand, Australia is home to a small population and is a vast, politically stable country with a still apparently unlimited potential for generating wealth. The lower value of the currency is creating new opportunities for exporters and local entrepreneurs involved in international markets. The tourist industry is also booming, as the world discovers that Australia offers the unique pleasures both of its sophisticated cities and of the remote, but increasingly accessible, wilderness areas of the dry outback, the tropical forests of the north, and the isolated mountains and valleys of the south.

The People and Their Culture

AUSTRALIANS ARE A MIXED BUNCH and it is hard to determine precisely the 'typical' national character. But the generations of settlers who adapted to and prospered in an often harsh new environment have created their own heroes.

Perhaps the image that Australians themelves are most fond of is the rugged bushman, product of the rough and usually isolated conditions that the predominantly male population had to endure during the last century. They were the cattle drovers, the sheep shearers and the gold diggers – practical men, rough and ready, and quick to debunk affectation. Always willing to 'have a go', they would attempt most things but had little compulsion to work hard without good reason.

They were also fiercely independent, sceptical of authority and relishing the freedom to come and go as they pleased. A man was as good as his word, no matter what his class or social ranking. Consequently he was a great 'knocker' of the eminent or the 'tall poppy' – especially intellectuals, politicians and the socialite – anyone who regarded himself as a cut above the common man. Yet the bushman's hospitality knew no bounds, and he would stick with his mates through thick and thin.

Perhaps the predominance of men in the early years of the colony led to an overly chauvinistic society. Women were outnumbered by as much as ten to one, an imbalance which continued until the second half of the last century, particularly in rural areas. Women were expected to fulfil many roles, from 'ministering angel' to model wives and mothers extending a civilising hand to smooth the uncouth edges of rough male society. Convict women often failed to meet this mythical standard as they struggled to survive the brutal realities of a penal settlement. This confused imagery of nineteenth century womanhood has been encapsulated by one Australian writer in the phrase 'damned whores and God's police'.

Contemporary Australians have inherited many of the characteristics of their forebears, despite having evolved into a highly urbanised society. Instead of the bush we have the 'great Aussie outdoors', which now encompasses the football or cricket field, or even the large backyard which is an integral part of most Australian homes. Rather than military, political or cultural figures, Australian heroes have often been sportsmen and women. Physical prowess, especially in team sports, is still regarded as an ultimate form of achievement.

The ideal of 'mateship' has also had a major impact on the shape of modern Australian society. At the end of the last century, as companies grew larger and opportunities for self-employment lessened, the collectivist ideals of working men grew naturally into a strong trade union movement. And while at times this has been a luxury the Australian economy could ill afford, it has also resulted in the creation of an effective welfare system.

A major new factor has entered the Australian cultural equation since the Second World War, with the changes that have occurred in traditional patterns of immigration. Although immigrants to Australia have long been drawn from many countries – Italians, for example, have been arriving since the early 1800s, Greeks since the 1850s, the Lebanese since the 1860s – European, and particularly British, settlers had predominated. Post-war immigration policies for the first time actively encouraged migrants from all over the world, and by the late 1960s the British intake had declined to less than half the annual total.

The newcomers have come from Italy, Greece, Germany, Yugoslavia, Turkey and Lebanon and, more recently, from South America, India, Hong Kong, Singapore and Vietnam, to name a few countries. Often they came to forget politics. Some came to better their own lives, but more often they came to better the lives of their children. And, generally, they have been prepared to work long hard hours to achieve their aims.

The effects have been profound. The more subtle changes have been at the cultural and political level. The most obvious has been the enriching of the Australian lifestyle. Many young Australians have completely abandoned the 'steak, eggs and chips' dietary regime of their parents and now enjoy a truly international cuisine. They have also adopted fashions which are more appropriate to the Australian climate and relaxed way of life.

But some uniquely Anglo-Saxon habits refuse to die out. On Christmas day, all around the country, when the summer temperatures are often way over 30°C, you can still smell the turkey roasting in the oven or taste a plum pudding steamed with its lucky silver coins. Afterwards, though, as the day cools towards evening, you will see kids and their parents outdoors playing cricket or touch football. And if you happen to wander past, you are sure to be greeted with that thoroughly Australian greeting, 'gidday mate'.

A Journey Around Australia

IT IS ITS CITIES AND TOWNS that perhaps best reflect the people and culture of modern Australia. If you were to get in a car and drive the 18 500 kilometres needed to circumnavigate the continent, you would experience a rare variety of people, climate and landforms.

Sydney

To make that imaginary journey, the best place to start would be Sydney, the country's largest city and, at 3.5 million, its most populous. It is generally regarded by other Australians — and even by many who live there — as a wild sprawling metropolis, flashy in the display of its wealth, and fast and frenetic in its manners and pastimes. It is a city where anything goes. Yet the people, like the city, can also be warm, friendly and fun loving. The one thing Sydneysiders hate is pretence — you are accepted for what you are, warts and all.

During the brilliant sunshine of summer, life revolves around Sydney's numerous beaches and backyard swimming pools. The focal point of the city itself is its magnificent yacht-studded harbour, overlooked by the elegant homes of the wealthy and dominated by its giant bridge and the famous Opera House beside it.

Travelling farther inland, a mass of red brick suburban houses carpets the landscape as the suburbs of Sydney expand ever westward towards the Blue Mountains. Our journey continues past these steep and magnificent ranges towards the southwest, until we come down to the grassy inland plains of the tablelands and the heart of the nation's valuable sheep industry. On our route we pass through many townships, for it was this region that saw the beginnings of Australian pastoralism.

Canberra

Continuing south we pass Australia's federal capital, Canberra, located about halfway

between Sydney and Melbourne and today a small but rapidly growing city of 250 000. Canberra was designed by an American architect, Walter Burley Griffin, in the early years of this century, although the federal parliament did not sit there until 1927. The skyline is now dominated by the new parliament house, open in 1988, the year of Australia's bicentennial celebrations.

Besides parliament, Canberra houses the Australian High Court, the War Museum, the National Library and the National Art Gallery, important symbols of Australia's nationhood. Yet the city itself has been described as soulless and dull, a town of bureaucrats, politicians and diplomats on an endless round of business lunches and cocktail parties. Architecturally it is an attractive town, one of the world's finest examples of a planned capital city. But, as an English writer once observed: 'Londoners may be all too aware of the disadvantages of living in a city without a plan, but they cannot be compared to the rival disadvantages of living in a plan without a city.'

From Canberra we skirt around the snowfields of the Southern Alps, cross the Murray River at Albury, and travel down through the rich agricultural heartland of Victoria until we reach its capital, Melbourne.

Melbourne

This old and comfortable city is renowned for its wet weather and cold winters. Trams still rumble through the flat and wide, tree-lined streets, designed originally so that livestock could be herded easily through the city to the docks. Care has also been taken to preserve the large old bluestone buildings of last century, which today stand alongside the city's gleaming new skyscrapers.

Melbourne is slightly smaller than Sydney, and its way of life slower and more leisurely – even, some would say, staid. Melbournites, however, claim to be more cultivated than their racy Sydney rivals. Melbourne is regarded by many as the political and cultural hub of the nation and it has long been prepared to nurture its artists and writers. In the past its intellectual tolerance resulted in some of Australia's finest schools and universities.

But there is another, more lively side to Melbourne, for it is the home of Australian Rules football, a derivative of an old Gaelic game imported by Irish gold-diggers. The names of the star players nowadays, however, are just as likely to be Greek or Italian as Irish. Every winter, as the season gears up for the grand finals, the footy crowds go into a frenzy, losing any semblance of that famous Melbourne reserve or decorum. The old town still knows how to let off steam.

From Melbourne we take an overnight ferry across the Bass Strait to Launceston, the second biggest town of the 'apple isle', Tasmania. Perhaps because of the colder climate and its isolation from the mainland, Tasmania has retained a more English flavour than the other states. As we head south towards its capital, Hobart, we pass numerous old stone farmhouses built by the convicts, as well as large apple orchards and fields of hops.

Hobart

Hobart, like the rest of the cities we shall visit, still has the feel of an overgrown country town. Perched on a natural harbour, and overshadowed by the forest-clad Mount Wellington, it is an easygoing city of 175 000 people. Its main claim to fame is as the finishing line for the Sydney to Hobart yacht race, which takes place annually between Christmas and New Year. The city has retained some of the air of a nineteenth century seaport, with old stone bondstores and warehouses still clustered around the harbour and along the colourful Salamanca Place. It also boasts one of Australia's longest established legal casino's, at Wrest Point.

Several hours out of Hobart we enter the huge wilderness areas of southwest Tasmania, a region which claims some of the oldest trees in the world. Many areas are so isolated and rough as to be inaccessible, but a well-developed network of hiking trails does provide the visitor with many chances for exploration.

We must return to the mainland before continuing around the rugged southern coastline of Victoria on our way to Adelaide. One of the country's most scenic routes, the Great Ocean Road, edges gigantic cliffs which sheer down into the large swells of the cold Southern Ocean. We pass the famous Twelve Apostles, wind-sculptured pinnacles of offshore rock which soar up to seventy metres above the battering waves.

Adelaide

As we approach Adelaide the lush pastures become drier and we enter the wheat and sheep country of South Australia. Adelaide is often described as the city of parks and churches — which gives an indication of its character. Convicts were never sent here, and strict social stratification and the protestant work ethic flourished. Until the 1970s it was considered the centre of one of the most conservative pastoral establishments in the land.

But Adelaide is today better known for its biennial festival of arts. For almost a month the city offers a feast of music, opera, ballet, theatre, art, literature and light entertainment, which attracts people both from interstate and overseas. Visitors often combine their stay with a trip to the beautiful Barossa Valley, where German settlers have been tending their vineyards since the 1840s. The area now produces about one third of Australia's wine.

From Adelaide we go north through more rolling wheat fields until we reach Port Augusta, a small but thriving industrial city at the head of the Spencer Gulf. Beyond us lies desert. We are about to take leave of the bustling eastern states and cross nearly 2500 kilometres of sand dunes and spinifex grasses until we reach the sanctuary of the prosperous west.

Here in the desert at night, under the clear star-studded sky, you can sometimes hear the earth rumbling as the waters flow through the huge artesian caverns underground. The Australian desert has an awesome beauty of its own. We will see plenty of it before we reach the end of our journey.

Perth

The first major signs of civilisation after we cross the Western Australian border are the twin goldmining towns of Kalgoorlie and Coolgardie. We are in the heart of what was once one of the world's richest goldfields, and mining for the precious metal has been going on here for over one hundred years. Also noticeable, for the first time, is the characteristic redness of the sand common to the west. It contains iron pyrites, the basis of iron ore, from which vast fortunes have been made farther to the north.

It isn't long before we enter wheat country again, before arriving in Perth. Despite being one of the most isolated cities in the world, it is a high-rolling town in every sense of the word. With a population of just under one million, it is like a smaller, more upmarket version of Sydney. Home to some of Australia's most famous and aggressive entrepreneurs, it is said you can almost smell the money in Perth.

Until the 1960s it was a small straggling city, often the first port of call for ships bringing migrants from Europe. But the discovery in the north of the state of huge quantities of iron ore and, more recently, oil and gas has since made this unlikely city very wealthy indeed. Perth is the financial and administrative hub of a state as large as western Europe, and it pulsates with the vigour of its new-found riches.

Perhaps the best symbol of Perth's new sense of self-confidence was its hosting in 1986–87 of the world's premier yacht race, the America's Cup, in the waters off the port city of Fremantle.

Perth itself boasts of the best climate in the country, with clear hot summers and cool wet winters. Its beaches and clear blue ocean are legendary. Within easy driving distance to the south are the rich farming and wine-growing areas around Margaret River, as well as the great karri forests which contain some of the tallest timber in the world. In the past, the timber industry played a major role in the state's economy.

To the north of Perth lies the port of Geraldton, and from then on we are entering one of Australia's last great frontiers. Although the vast northwest has been sparcely settled by cattle-station owners for over a century, the discovery of minerals and oil is rapidly opening up the whole area, and an all-weather bitumen road linking Perth to Darwin has recently been completed. Before this, coastal settlements relied on supply boats for provisions.

The old pearling town of Broome is probably the highlight of any visit to the northwest.

Since the last century, master pearlers and divers, including many from Japan and Southeast Asia, have used Broome as a base for their operations. In many ways it still retains aspects of a colonial outpost in the tropics, although tourism is making rapid inroads into this unique multiracial town and replacing the dying pearling trade as its main source of income. Its beaches are superb, the fishing excellent, and the convergence on Broome every Friday night of cowboys and roughnecks after weeks of isolation in the desert gives the town a perpetual party atmosphere.

Darwin

Another 1000 kilometres to the north is Darwin, the capital and administrative centre of the Northern Territory. The city was flattened by a cyclone which hit on Christmas Day 1974, and has since been completely rebuilt. A town with a tropical climate, it swelters in the summer but has the best winter climate in Australia.

Darwin serves as a centre for the rapidly developing pastoral and mining industries of the north. It is also an important tourist centre, a base for exploration of the wild and fascinating country of the 'Top End'. The people are typical of Australia's more remote areas – easygoing, with something of the old frontier spirit.

The next stop 'down the track', as the Territorians say, is 1200 kilometres to the south. Alice Springs is at the geographical heart of the nation, and the departure point for those wishing to visit Australia's most famous landmark, Ayers Rock. The Alice itself is a beautiful town, the greenery of the gardens and the shady ghost gums lining the streets contrasting with the harsh desert which surrounds it. It has become one of the the country's most popular tourist destinations for those wishing to travel outback, and many of the former shanties have given way to modern hotels and motels, shops, restaurants and art galleries.

It is the desert that most come to visit, harsh and yet incredibly beautiful with its rolling waves of red and purple colour, deep chasms containing surprisingly lush tropical plants and freshwater pools, and bizarre and lonely rock formations.

From here we must backtrack across the desolate north of the continent until we again reach the green east coast and the thriving city of Townsville in northern Queensland. Attractively situated on the side of a small mountain, this friendly city is a gateway to the treasures of the tropical north and the famed Great Barrier Reef, which stretches for 2000 kilometres along the Queensland coast.

Among the tough pioneers who originally settled the area were many Italian sugarcane and tobacco growers. Although these are still thriving industries when market prices are high, they have been overshadowed by the tourist and development boom which has recently enveloped the area. It is easy to understand why. Northern Queensland is a rich tropical paradise, with palm-fringed beaches of white sand, coral reefs, and exotic rainforests. The beautiful islands of the Whitsunday group are an idyllic haven for visitors with an interest in yachting and underwater exploration.

Brisbane

Over 1500 kilometres to the south is the Queensland state capital, Brisbane, a sprawling relaxed city of 1.2 million inhabitants. Some of the grand old colonial buildings with their wide verandahs and high ceilings still exist, now lined up next to gleaming, airconditioned skyscrapers. The city is renowned for its colourful parks and gardens, which flourish in its subtropical climate.

To complete this grand circumnavigation of the continent we must continue south through the bustling Gold Coast and the city of Surfers Paradise. This area is traditionally a mecca for southern holidaymakers and is now full of towering holiday apartments, restaurants and nightclubs and, of course, great stretches of golden beaches.

Farther south we pass through the canefields, dairy farms and banana plantations of the densely populated north coast of New South Wales, skirt the vineyards of the Hunter Valley and the giant steelworks of Newcastle, and finally reach Sydney once again.

Few countries in the world can compete with the diverse attractions of Australia, the greatness of its wilderness areas and the sheer size of that everpresent cobalt-blue sky.

The Land, its Flora and Fauna

THE AUSTRALIAN CONTINENT sits astride the Tropic of Capricorn in majestic isolation between two of the world's great oceans, the Indian and the Pacific.

At 7 682 300 square kilometres, its area is nearly equal to the mainland states of the United States, excluding Alaska, and thirty-two times greater than the United Kingdom. The distance between Sydney on the east coast, and Perth on the west, is similar to that between London and Moscow. Australia has gentle rolling hills reminiscent of old England, snow-covered mountain peaks, vine festooned rainforests and the burning sands of only marginally explored deserts.

The Great Dividing Range, which was formed by a momentous wrinkling in the earth's crust many millions of years ago, sweeps down the eastern flank of the continent, effectively splitting it in two. Between the Pacific Ocean and these mountains are the lush coastal plains where most Australians live, including the city dwellers of Brisbane, Sydney and Melbourne. To the west of the Great Divide lie the drier desert areas, including the western plateau which continues virtually uninterrupted to the Indian Ocean.

Australia is the flattest continent in the world, and the driest: 60 per cent of the country is arid, receiving less than 400 millimetres per year.

Australia's size gives it a varied climate, but one without great extremes. Slightly more than half of Queensland, a third of Western Australia and 80 per cent of the Northern Territory lie within the tropical zone. Here the summer season or 'Wet' occurs between November and April, bringing with it monsoon rains, thunderstorms and the occasional tropical cyclone, while humidity remains high and temperatures are between 33°C and 36°C.

Central and southern Queensland are subtropical. Farther south are the warm temperate regions of New South Wales, South Australia and Western Australia. The coolest areas are Victoria, southwest Western Australia and Tasmania. In all these regions spring and summer are in September to February, and autumn and winter in March to August, but without the sharply distinguished seasonal changes of Europe and North America.

From east to west the contrasts are just as marked. The eastern coast is lined with hundreds of kilometres of wide beaches, river estuaries and inland waterways. The rich and fertile coastal soil is heavily timbered by eucalypt and acacia woodlands, with pockets of rainforest. Much of the original tree cover has long since been cleared for sugarcane and tropical fruits and, farther south, pasture for dairy herds.

Farther inland the rolling hazy blue mountains begin to rise. In many areas small creeks converge into swift sharp rivers, cutting magnificent ravines across the rainforested eastern escarpments and pouring water down across the coast and into the sea. Too steep to be farmed, the mountains are still the domain of bushwalkers, and much of Australia's unique flora and fauna. To the south the mountains rise to their highest point of 2228 metres at Mount Kosciusko in the highlands of New South Wales. Snow covers these mountains from June to October, attracting ski enthusiasts to many resorts.

On the other side of the Great Divide the land slopes gently towards the west. Here are more open eucalypt forests, drier than on the coast, with lazy brown tree-lined rivers which meander slowly to the south and west. This is Australia's rich agricultural heartland, where sheep and cattle have been grazed for over a century and a huge wheat-growing industry has developed.

Then the rivers dry into channels which flow only after heavy rain. For over a century cattlemen have grazed their stock here on huge stations which in the north can cover millions of hectares and have traditionally been measured in square miles rather than acres.

The flat salt-bush plains give way to sandhills, and trees become a rarity. This is the desolate outback, its vastness broken only by the huge craggy rock formations of ancient mountain ranges. Finally, more than 2000 kilometres to the west, vegetation appears again before the land is abruptly halted by the Indian Ocean.

The Flora

Australia's long continental isolation has resulted in a vegetation which differs markedly from that of the rest of the world. At first sight the Australian bush can be monotonous and intimidating, until one comes to realise its subtle adaptation to the parched conditions of the land.

The hardy eucalypt or gum tree, that stalwart symbol of the Australian bush, is perhaps the best example. To conserve their internal moisture, eucalypts turn their leaves so that only the edge and not the flat leaf surface is facing the hot sun, indeed their characteristic greyness is due to a protective coating against evaporation. Eucalypts, like many other species of Australian flora, have also adapted to the dangerous bushfires which are a part of every Australian summer. Many need fire or similar wide destruction in order to regenerate.

The tremendous variety of flora has developed from three main sources. The Indo–Malayan element is found in the tropical and subtropical rainforest and monsoon habitats of northern Australia, where there has been plant migration from Southeast Asia. There is also the southern or Antarctic vegetation, which includes many plants related to those of New Zealand, South Africa and South America. The purely Australian element has evolved since the continent separated from Antarctica over 45 million years ago.

Australian vegetation is almost entirely evergreen. There are no extensive deciduous forests, and only small areas of conifers. The landscape is dominated by two easily recognisable types of tree – the eucalypts or gum trees, and the acacias or wattles.

At the last count 550 different species of eucalypt had been identified. They vary from the tall, straight timbers of the eastern forests, to the low clumpy mallees of drier areas. The best known are from two extremes of climate – the smooth-barked snow gum, which stands gnarled and twisted at the very highest limit of growth in the Australian Alps; and the ghost gum, whose stark white trunk contrasts so vividly with the red soil of the inland.

Acacias also come in many shapes and sizes, from small ground-hugging shrubs to tall trees. There are over 700 species, which flower mainly in late winter, bearing a mass of button-sized cream and yellow-gold flowers. Some have feathery leaves, others flat stalk-like phyllodes.

Australia has many thousands of species of flowering plants. The beautiful wildflowers of the coastal sand plains and the Stirling Range of Western Australia are particularly magnificent in spring, especially following good winter rains.

Forests

The dank and brooding rainforests of the northeastern coast are densely foliaged, with tall trees of various species. Huge woody vines twist high up around tree trunks and loop down from lower branches, and beautiful orchids and ferns such as elkhorns abound. Eucalypts do not grow in rainforests, and the large red cedar and Queensland maple trees which thrive in the moist conditions have been logged out in many areas because of their excellent quality as cabinet timbers.

Around the rainforests lie forests of tall straight-trunked eucalypts, with usually one or two species dominant in any area. The giant mountain ashes are perhaps the most spectacular, and they are an impressive sight when festooned with their long strips of deciduous bark.

*E*mus

The Australian Alps

In the alpine regions of southern New South Wales, Victoria and Tasmania the dominant trees are snow gums. These stunted hardy trees consist of several slender trunks rising from ground level. Above the tree line, at about 1800 metres, ground-hugging shrubs and meadows of grass and herbs predominate. Flowering comes later, away from the warmer coastal regions, and summer produces magnificent swathes of flowers of virtually every colour.

Grasses and Woodlands

These areas occur farther to the west of the dense coastal forests, across the broad tropical belt of northern Australia and in the continent's southwest corner. In the north, much of the woodland consists of more openly spaced eucalypts, with the dominant trees rising to thirty metres. The underlayer usually contains bushes and coarse grasses which grow in tall dense swards after the summer monsoons. There are also some deciduous trees, including the tall bombax or red cotton tree, which sheds its leaves in the dry season and then forms a blaze of red flowers before the foliage appears for the Wet. Australia's most famous deciduous tree is the baobab, with white flowers and an enormous bottled-shaped trunk.

The open woodlands of the southeast and southwest regions are also mainly made up of eucalypts, with trees such as the majestic red river gum lining the banks of the major inland rivers. Native pines predominate in areas such as the Flinders Ranges of South Australia, and the Pilliga Scrub of western New South Wales. The many species of shrub include the emu bush with its showy tubular flowers of white, pink, purple and red.

Mallee and Mulga

Two distinctively Australian types of drought-resistant woodland occur in the more arid mainland regions. 'Mallee' is a term given to areas dominated by low-growing eucalypts with several slender stems rising from a single rootstock. These trees are found in a band across the semi-arid areas of the south. Mulga occurs in even drier areas. A bushy grey-green acacia, it grows to between five and ten metres in height.

The trees of these regions are sparsely planted in dry sandy soils. Rain is infrequent but heavy falls are followed by a spectacular burst of flowering, as small soft-stemmed ground orchids, daisies and other herbaceous plants germinate, grow, seed and die within a few weeks. In areas where trees are sparse or absent, tussocky grasses provide valuable cattle fodder.

The Desert

In this harshest of environments, the sand dunes are usually devoid of vegetation or have only a sparse cover of spinifex grass. The troughs between the dunes sometimes contain dwarfed trees or shrubs. But heavy rains bring the desert to life, and a herbaceous flora similar to that of the drier woodlands and mulga country erupts in a burst of colour and completes its cycle in a few weeks.

The arid zone of central Australia is one of the largest in the world and consists of stony deserts called gibber plains, and sandy deserts containing long parallel ridges or crescent-shaped dunes. Temperatures there rise to above 40°C in midsummer, but drop below freezing at night. Rainfall may be less than 150 millimetres a year.

Lakes and Rivers

Much of Australia's arid zone is without rivers, but in the east there are rivers which flow only after heavy rains. Around the coast, short rivers rise in the mountains and flow swiftly to the sea, many with beautiful waterfalls which drop sharply into clear pools. Inland rivers are wide, twisting, muddy and slow moving.

The rivers and fresh or saltwater lakes, swamps, saline flats and claypans of Australia usually support specialised and often beautiful vegetation. Tropical rivers and lakes are fringed with tall paperbarks and pandanus. Freshwater lagoons are replenished each monsoon season and support an abundant growth of colourful waterlilies and other aquatic plants. The low estuaries and mudflats of the Queensland coast support an astonishing variety of autumn-flowering mangroves.

Fauna

Australia's rich and fascinating animal life is world famous and again largely reflects its long geographical isolation. Unfortunately, early European settlers were quick to exploit the abundance of native animals for their furs and skins, and later had little hesitation in attempting to eradicate those which threatened crops and pasture.

The native dog, the dingo, has never been accepted by Australian farmers and many still die painful deaths by poison or the shotgun. In the 1930s machine-guns were used to cull large flocks of the flightless emu, and today kangaroos are culled to protect grazing pastures and provide meat for a growing pet-food industry. The introduced animals such as rabbits, foxes, deer and rats have also caused long-term problems.

Since the development of a broadly based conservation movement, however, most Australians are now taking a more enlightened approach to the environment, and attempts are being made to balance the needs of farmers with those of Australia's unique and remarkable fauna. Today, over 30 million hectares of land are set aside as national parks and nature conservation areas, in addition to the declaration of several marine parks offshore.

Birds

The Australian bush is renowned for its prolific birdlife. The open forests of the east coast abound with the delightful bellbird, whose ringing call echoes through the tall-timbered ranges. The kookaburra is another Australian favourite, with its raucous laugh-like call. And also the lyrebird, well known for its remarkable gauzy tail and the male's elaborate dancing display. Australian pelicans are a familar sight in coastal waters. They fish cooperatively, with six to eight birds swimming in a circle to form a living net.

There are over fifty colourful species of parrot, ranging from small nectar-feeders to the large and heavy bodied, seed-eating cockatoos.

Each Australian state and territory has a bird as its emblem. Western Australia's is the black swan, a unique bird and the continent's only swan. The country's largest bird of prey, the wedge-tailed eagle, is that of the Northern Territory. Australia's unofficial bird emblem is the emu, a large flightless bird which can run at up to sixty kilometres an hour and which inhabits the drier mainland areas.

Reptiles

Australia's largest reptiles are the salt and freshwater crocodiles of the tropical north. The smaller, freshwater crocodile is a fairly harmless species which feeds mainly on tortoises. Saltwater crocodiles, however, have been recorded at seven metres long and can pose considerable danger to unsuspecting swimmers.

There are also many species of marine and freshwater turtle, as well as lizards and snakes. Australia has about 360 species of lizard ranging in size from the tiny garden skink to the giant perentie of the arid northern and central regions, which can grow to 2.4 metres. The most bizarre are probably the thorny devil or moloch, which is covered with a skin armour of many large spines, and the frill-necked lizard, whose name comes from the spectacular ruff it displays when attacked. Australia has no venomous lizards, but many of its 140 snake species are deadly. Fortunately most of these are not aggressive and usually disappear at the approach of humans.

Mammals

Probably the most bizarre and interesting of Australia's native animals are the two monotremes, the platypus and and echidna. These are the world's only egg-laying mammals. The platypus is a fur-covered water dweller, with webbed clawed feet and a duck-like bill. It is found only in the rivers and lakes of eastern Australia, where it feeds on crustaceans, worms and other small invertebrates. Much of its life is spent in a burrow excavated in the bank of a river or stream. Unfortunately, like many Australian mammals, its fur was greatly prized by early settlers and the species nearly became extinct through trapping. Now, however, it is protected by law.

The echidna, or spiny anteater, lives on land and mainly eats ants and termites, which it gathers up with its long and sticky, ribbon-like tongue. It has no teeth and relies on its coat of stiff spines for protection. When alarmed, it uses its sharp claws to dig into the ground.

The majority of Australian mammals are marsupials, most but not all of which carry their young in a pouch. The young of marsupials are born at an extremely immature stage – blind, hairless and without hind legs – and must attach themselves to the mother's teat to continue their development.

Perhaps the most famous marsupial is Australia's national emblem, the kangaroo. There are forty-five species of kangaroo in Australia, ranging in size from the tiny musk rat-kangaroo, which is less than thirty centimetres long and lives in the Atherton Tableland of the north Queensland coast, to the giant red kangaroo of the western plains. Male reds may weigh around eighty-five kilograms and stand over two metres tall.

Another well-known Australian mammal is the koala, which lives in the eucalypt forests of eastern Australia. This furry, bear-like creature feeds only on the young leaves of certain eucalypts. In spite of its size (about seventy-five centimetres long), it is difficult to spot during the daytime because this is when it sleeps, high up in the trees.

The greatest problem in observing Australian mammals in their native state is that most are solitary, inconspicuous, and nocturnal. The generally warm to hot climate demands that animals remain quiet and sheltered during the daytime to conserve their body water. However, most can be seen in Australia's many informative and well-designed zoos, while the visitor to a national park at dusk may have some exciting and unusual encounters.

Natural Wonders

TIME HAS PROVIDED the Australian continent with some spectacular geological structures. The combined effects of wind, sand and water have created these natural masterpieces, whose unique beauty adds even greater depth to the beauty of the Australian landscape.

The Great Barrier Reef

The Great Barrier Reef is the largest structure ever built by living organisms. It stretches for over 2000 kilometres from the Torres Strait to the coast of central Queensland. It is dotted with hundreds of beautiful islands, many of which are the peaks of submerged mountains. Some are hilly, with fresh water and large trees, while others are no more than sandy outcrops. Much of the reef has been declared national park, although several islands have secluded facilities for tourists.

The coral polyp which creates the reef is a tiny animal related to the sea anemones. It excretes lime, which forms the basis of the reef. The beautifully coloured outer coral is made up of millions of the living polyps, below which lies the older limestone base. The 350 or so species of coral range in colour from soft pinks to purples, blues, crimson, fawn, yellow and deep browns. Some are shaped like staghorns with great antlers, others are like delicate trees.

And then there are the brilliantly decorated fish – parrot fish, angel fish, coral trout, the venomous although beautiful butterfly cod – as well as turtles and sea snakes, giant rays, sharks and marlin, the giant purple-lipped clams and the delicate anemones.

It is not possible to see the reefs from the mainland beaches because they lie well out from the coast – at its southern end the reef is up to 300 kilometres away from the mainland, but it is closer in the north. However, the island resorts make the reef more accessible – two of them, Green Island and Heron Island, are coral cays and part of the reef itself – while passenger cruises, charter yachts and launches are available from mainland centres such as Rockhampton, Mackay and Cairns. The best way to see the reef, of course, is by scubadiving or from a glass-bottomed boat. Green Island, which is only twenty-seven kilometres from Cairns and reached by a fast hydrofoil service, has an underwater observatory.

Ayers Rock

The Rock has been described as the world's largest pebble and, indeed, it rises 348 metres into the sky above a flat and featureless desert plain, while it is a five-hour walk

The 'Twelve Apostles'
at sunset, Victoria

of almost nine kilometres around its base. It is located at virtually the dead centre of the continent and is one of the Australian Aborigines' most sacred sites. The beauty of the rock must be seen to be believed, as its colour changes from the greyish purple of early morning to the reds and deep ochre of the late afternoon.

About thirty kilometres to the west are the Olgas, a cluster of smaller, more rounded rocks. Here there are many walking trails, as well as valleys and quiet shady pools to explore.

Tourists are well catered for with hotels, shops and an information centre at the Yulara resort, which is located just outside the national park only eighteen kilometres from the Rock. The nearest town, Alice Springs, is 448 kilometres away, and from there visits can also be made to the Macdonnell Ranges where rivers have cut magnificent chasms through the stark rock chains. Deep in these gorges are beautiful waterholes with tall graceful palms offering a calm contrast to the harshness of the surrounding desert.

Tasmania's Southwestern Wilderness

Few places are as isolated, or so beautiful and wild as Tasmania's southwest. Only recently has it achieved official recognition as one of the world's last great frontiers, largely due to the efforts of environmentalists who fought so hard to preserve it from those who wished to dam its mighty rivers and log its ancient timbers.

This is country that has changed little since the ice age and which contains some of the oldest trees and most primitive plant life in the world. Man is still only a guest in its environs: tracks are few, the weather capricious, and the going usually tough. But the rewards for those who meet the challenge are great. This region is home to the Huon pine which lives for over 2000 years. Here are also some of the earth's last tracts of virgin temperate rainforest, where huge trees are festooned with delicate mosses and lichen. On higher ground, superb glacial tarns and alpine meadows decorate the saw-toothed mountains.

The wild rivers shoot down spectacularly narrow ravines and over immense rapids. Many are suitable for rafting or canoeing, but only in the company of experienced guides.

The Western Wildflowers

Every year from September to November, the wildflowers of southwest Western Australia carpet the landscape in delicate profusion. Vividly blue leschenaultia, spiky green and red kangaroo paws, and orange-gold banksias give brilliant displays, while the brown boronia perfumes the air.

The western deserts will also bloom after heavy rain, as countless small annuals germinate, covering the sandhills with a mass of colour. Among the most spectacular are the scarlet and black Sturt's desert pea, named for the inland explorer Charles Sturt; and the pink, yellow or white everlasting daisies which may cover hundreds of square kilometres for several weeks at a time.

The Great Dividing Range

This massive sweep of mountains stretches over 3500 kilometres from the north to the south of the continent. Among its natural wonders are the unique tropical rainforests of northern Queensland, the Glasshouse mountains farther to the south of the state (whose glass-smooth rocks shimmer in the way their name suggests), the magnificent waterfalls of the rugged New England ranges, and the massive sandstone ranges of Victoria's west, named the Grampians by an early explorer in memory of his native Scotland.

But overlooking the country's most populous city, Sydney, and only two hours drive from its heart, are the stunning Blue Mountains, so called because of the vivid blue haze which hangs above them. The mountains are broken by vast wooded valleys and precipitous gorges, waterfalls, caves and unusual rock formations. Hundreds of well-marked bushwalking tracks take travellers deep into the beautiful valleys and seemingly light years away from the bustle of the twentieth century.

Another eighty kilometres to the southwest are a series of majestic limestone caves. Legend has it that the first European to visit the Jenolan caves was a convict turned bushranger who used them as a hideout. They have been open to the public for the last 120 years, although parts of the complex have still not been explored. The caves were formed thousands of years ago by water erosion of underground streams, and contain spectacular stalactites and stalagmites. They are surrounded by a wildlife reserve with extensive nature trails where walkers may spot a wallaby or a possum, or even the elusive lyrebird.

Modern transport has given the visitor access to most of Australia's special places, yet the unique sense of a vast and timeless landscape has been preserved.

Information for Visitors

FOR TRAVELLERS TO AUSTRALIA a valid passport is necessary, and visitors of all nationalities (except holders of Australian and New Zealand passports) must obtain a visa before arrival. These are available at Australian embassies, high commissions or consulate offices listed in local telephone directories. Other requirements for entry are a return or onward passenger ticket and evidence of sufficient funds for the period of stay. Health certificates are not required unless arriving from an area infected by yellow fever, smallpox, cholera or typhoid.

Newcomers may be surprised to find that when their aircraft lands in Australia, the interior will be sprayed as a control against insects. This is because Australia is free from many exotic pests and diseases. The import of all foodstuffs, plants and plant products is also strictly controlled.

Currency

The Australian currency is decimal, with the dollar as the basic unit. Notes come in a colourful array of $100, $50, $20, $10, $5 and $2 denominations, with minted coins for lesser amounts including the gold $1 coin. There is no limit on personal funds when entering the country and visitors may leave with whatever they brought in, but with no more than $5000 in notes and coins in Australian currency.

Currency exchange facilities are available at international airports, and most banks and large hotels.

Air Travel

Because of the vast distances and often harsh climate, Australia has benefited more than most countries from modern transport systems. Air travel, in particular, has helped open up the more remote regions of the country, and in outback areas it is not uncommon to see a cowboy in jeans check in his saddle and swag and settle down for the flight next to an executive in a business suit.

Because the benefits of air transport were recognised early on, a comprehensive network of domestic and international services has been developed, with one of the best safety records in the world.

Qantas, the country's international airline with the distinctive kangaroo emblem on the tail of its planes, is one of the oldest airlines in existence. From a single aeroplane operating in outback Queensland during the early 1920s, Qantas now maintains a fleet of Boeing 747 and 767 jets which fly to thirty-nine cities and twenty-four countries, with more than

Cedar Creek,
Queensland

100 flights in and out of Australia every week.

Three major domestic airlines – Australian Airlines, Ansett Airlines and East-West Airlines – operate jet services between capital cities, regional centres and resort areas throughout Australia. Regional airlines also exist which provide scheduled services from capital cities and provincial centres not served by the major airlines, as well as operating feeder services to the main domestic trunk routes.

Because of the distances that often have to be travelled, domestic airfares are generally more expensive than those of many other countries. However, overseas visitors are eligible for generous discount rates and special airfares which are available through travel agents and international airline offices.

Bus services operate between major airports and cities. Taxi cabs and rental cars are also available at all airports, although it is best to reserve rental cars in advance.

Rail Travel

One of the most cost-effective and scenic ways to travel in Australia is by train. It's a great way to meet other Australians, and there are few places you cannot reach by this tried and trusted method. The *Indian Pacific* crosses the continent from Sydney to Perth and is one of the great railway journeys of the world.

Modern interstate trains link all the major cities, from Perth in the west to Cairns in the far north of Queensland, and from Adelaide to the heart of the outback at Alice Springs. State railway networks also service provincial cities and rural areas.

Rail services in Australia are well patronised, so it is advisable to book in advance. An Austrail pass allows unlimited travel for visitors, at very reasonable rates.

Motoring

Travelling by car is also an ideal way to see Australia, allowing you to explore near and far, stopping whenever and wherever you wish. Australians drive on the left-hand side of the road, like the British and the Japanese. Speed and distances are in kilometres, although traffic signs conform to international standards and are easy to read. A vehicle may be driven with a driver's licence valid in the visitor's home country.

Each state has its own motoring organisation (affiliated with those in other states so that membership of only one is necessary), which provides touring information, maps, travel publications, emergency breakdown services, and travel agency assistance.

Rental cars are available at major air and rail terminals, from central city locations, and in many resort areas throughout Australia. Quite a few companies are in the field and rates are competitive, so it is worth shopping around for a good deal. Campervans and motorhomes are also available for rental, giving the traveller flexibility and independence.

Visitors with time on their hands can travel

extensively using express coach services. Coaches are air-conditioned, with headrests and adjustable seats, and most with a washroom–toilet. They are probably the cheapest way to see Australia, and departure points are clean, safe and conveniently located. The major interstate motorcoach companies include Ansett Pioneer, Greyhound Australia and Deluxe Coachlines.

Camping Tours and Safaris

An organised camping safari in a go-anywhere vehicle is an ideal way to visit the more remote and exotic parts of the country. It is especially suitable for those who enjoy being part of a team, in a tenting adventure hundreds of kilometres from 'civilisation'.

The most popular tours are in the eight to twenty-one day range, although they can be longer, or as short as a weekend. There are no age barriers either – all you need is a sense of adventure and a love of the great outdoors.

In recent years this form of travel has become very popular for Australians and visitors alike. A number of companies specialise in these trips, and information about them is available through most travel agencies, state government travel centres, or offices of the Australian Tourism Commission.

Accommodation

Australia has well-developed hotel and motel accomodation in cities, resorts and rural areas. A typical room is usually spotlessly clean, and has air-conditioning, a private bathroom, tea and coffee making facilities, a telephone, television and a small refrigerator. Because of the climate, many hotels and motels have small outdoor swimming pools.

Although the rooms are often the same, there is a difference between a hotel and a motel in Australia. A hotel must have a public bar among its facilities; motels often provide a bar for paying guests and invited friends, although they are not obliged to do this. Most hotels and motels have a dining room or restaurant.

First class hotels include names familar throughout the world – branches of the Hilton, Sheraton, Regent International, Hyatt and Intercontinental can be found in all of Australia's major cities.

Motels have generally been developed to meet the needs of travelling motorists and are located in cities, towns and resorts, and along major highways.

Youth hostels offer an inexpensive alternative to budget-conscious travellers in most parts of the country, with fees varying from $4 to $8 a night. Membership of the International or Australian Youth Hostel Federation is required.

Most towns and holiday resorts also have caravan parks and camping grounds with shower and toilet facilities, at very reasonable rates.

Climate

It is important when planning any trip to take account of the weather. Fortunately, the Australian climate is generally pleasant and without extremes in temperature. The seasons are opposite to those of the northern hemisphere, with spring from September to November, summer from December to February, autumn from March to May, and winter from June to August. The southern half of the continent experiences all four seasons, with cool to mild winters in coastal regions accompanied by some rain, but usually clear and sunny. Snow occurs only on the high mountain areas. Summer is warm to hot in the temperate south, with temperatures usually modified along the coast by fresh sea breezes.

The northern tropics have two seasons, the summer 'Wet' and the winter 'Dry'. The Wet is extremely hot and humid, and can be unpleasant for those unused to it. In some remote areas, travellers can be trapped for weeks by floodwaters if air transport is not available. Obviously the ideal time for travelling in these areas is during the Dry, which corresponds to the winter months in the south.

Further Information

For more information about Australia a trip to the local bookshop or library should reveal some publications about the general history, culture and people of this intriguing land. More detailed information can be sought from an Australian embassy or high commission in a capital city. International travel agencies should also prove helpful, while the Australian Tourist Commission has overseas offices and offers numerous publications about the country.

And, of course, holidaying Australians will always be a good source of information – they'll probably tell you they can't wait to get back home!

*One of
Sydney's symbols at sunset,
the Harbour Bridge*

*A*yers Rock at sunset

Photograph by Steven Dunbar